500 Insp̲ Quotes by Maya Angelou about success, Education and Life

PUBLISHED by: Scriptum Books

Table of Contents

Introduction..3

Maya Angelou: A Life of Resilience, Creativity, and Influence 5

500 Inspirational Quotesby Maya Angelou...............................9

Afterword..149

Book from the Same Author..................................151

Introduction

Maya Angelou, a name that resonates with wisdom, resilience, and a deep understanding of the human experience, has inspired millions across the globe with her profound words. A poet, memoirist, and civil rights activist, Angelou's work transcends the boundaries of time and culture, offering insights that are as relevant today as they were when first written. Her voice, both powerful and compassionate, continues to guide those seeking inspiration in their journeys of success, education, and life.

This book, "500 Inspirational Quotes by Maya Angelou about Success, Education, and Life," is a carefully curated collection of her most impactful statements. Each quote embodies Angelou's unique perspective, drawn from her rich and varied experiences—from her early struggles to her eventual rise as a literary icon. These quotes not only encapsulate the essence of her wisdom but also serve as a source of motivation and reflection for readers of all ages.

Success, as Angelou often reminds us, is not merely about achieving wealth or recognition. It is about finding purpose, embracing one's identity, and persevering in the face of adversity. Her insights into education emphasize the power of knowledge and the importance of lifelong learning, urging us to never stop questioning, growing, and seeking truth. And when it comes to life, Angelou's words offer a roadmap for living with grace, dignity, and authenticity.

As you turn the pages of this book, you will find quotes that inspire courage, encourage introspection, and foster a deeper appreciation for the complexities of life. Whether you are at the beginning of your journey or looking for guidance along the way, these words from Maya Angelou will serve as a beacon of hope and strength.

Let this collection be a companion to you, a reminder that success is within your reach, education is your lifelong ally, and life, with all its challenges and triumphs, is a gift to be cherished.

Maya Angelou: A Life of Resilience, Creativity, and Influence

Maya Angelou, born Marguerite Annie Johnson on April 4, 1928, in St. Louis, Missouri, emerged as one of the most influential voices of the 20th and early 21st centuries. Her life and work, marked by a profound commitment to truth, justice, and artistic expression, left an indelible mark on literature, civil rights, and the global cultural landscape.

Early Life and Challenges

Angelou's early years were fraught with hardship. Her parents' marriage ended when she was very young, and she and her older brother, Bailey, were sent to live with their grandmother in Stamps, Arkansas. The racial discrimination and segregation that permeated the South during this time deeply affected her. A traumatic experience at the age of eight, where she was sexually abused by her mother's boyfriend, led to years of selective mutism, during which Angelou spoke only to her brother.

Despite these early challenges, Angelou developed a love for literature and the arts, finding solace in books and the works of authors like William Shakespeare, Charles Dickens, and Edgar Allan Poe. Her passion for learning and self-expression would later become central themes in her writing.

Rise to Prominence

As a young adult, Angelou embarked on a series of jobs that reflected her adventurous spirit and drive. She worked as a cook, streetcar conductor, and nightclub performer, among other roles. During this time, she adopted the stage name Maya Angelou, a combination of her childhood nickname and a variation of her first husband's surname.

Her breakthrough came with the publication of her first autobiography, I Know Why the Caged Bird Sings (1969). This poignant and powerful memoir chronicles her early life, including the trauma she endured and her eventual path to self-discovery. The book was an instant success, earning critical acclaim and establishing Angelou as a significant literary voice. It also marked the beginning of a series of autobiographical works that would span her life, each exploring different aspects of her experiences.

Literary and Artistic Contributions

Maya Angelou's literary output was vast and varied. She authored seven autobiographies, several volumes of poetry, essays, plays, and even cookbooks. Her poetry, known for its lyrical beauty and emotional depth, often dealt with themes of identity, race, and resilience. One of her most famous poems, "Still I Rise," encapsulates her indomitable spirit and has become a rallying cry for those facing oppression.

In addition to her writing, Angelou was a talented performer and a gifted orator. She acted in plays and films, directed productions, and even recorded albums. Her 1993 recitation of her poem "On the Pulse of Morning" at the inauguration of President Bill Clinton brought her work to a global audience, earning her widespread recognition and respect.

Civil Rights Activism

Throughout her life, Angelou was deeply involved in the civil rights movement. She worked closely with both Martin Luther King Jr. and Malcolm X, using her talents to support the fight for racial equality. Her activism was not limited to the United States; she spent time in Ghana and Egypt, where she connected with other prominent African and African American intellectuals and artists.

Angelou's work as an activist informed much of her writing. Her ability to articulate the struggles and aspirations of African Americans with such clarity and compassion made her a beloved figure in the civil rights community and beyond.

Legacy and Impact

Maya Angelou's influence extended far beyond her literary achievements. She was a professor, mentor, and cultural ambassador who inspired generations of writers, artists, and activists. Her message of hope, perseverance, and the importance of self-worth resonated with people from all walks of life.

In her later years, Angelou received numerous honors, including the Presidential Medal of Freedom in 2011, awarded by President Barack Obama. Her legacy continues to live on through her works, which remain essential reading for anyone seeking to understand the complexities of the human experience.

Maya Angelou passed away on May 28, 2014, at the age of 86. Her life was a testament to the power of resilience, the importance of speaking one's truth, and the enduring impact of art and activism. Today, she is remembered not only as a literary giant but also as a symbol of strength, courage, and the enduring human spirit.

"Nothing will work unless you do."

"All great achievements require time."

"People will forget what you said, people will forget what you did, but people will never forget how you made them feel."

"Do the best you can until you know better. Then when you know better, do better."

"Success is liking yourself, liking what you do, and liking how you do it."

"If you are always trying to be normal, you will never know how amazing you can be."

"Never make someone a priority when all you are to them is an option."

"Nothing can dim the light which shines from within."

"Talent is like electricity. We don't understand electricity. We use it."

"When someone shows you who they are believe them; the first time."

"Try to be a rainbow in someone's cloud."

"Live as though life was created for you."

"If you don't like something, change it. If you can't change it, change your attitude."

"You can't use up creativity. The more you use, the more you have."

"There is no greater agony than bearing an untold story inside you."

"Ask for what you want and be prepared to get it."

"When you do nothing you feel overwhelmed and powerless. But when you get involved you feel the sense of hope and accomplishment that comes from knowing you are working to make things better."

"My mission in life is not merely to survive, but to thrive; and to do so with some passion, some compassion, some humor, and some style."

"You can only become truly accomplished at something you love. Don't make money your goal. Instead pursue the things you love doing and then do them so well that people can't take their eyes off of you."

"Success is loving life and daring to live it."

"You can't really know where you are going until you know where you have been."

"At the end of the day people won't remember what you said or did, they will remember how you made them feel."

"The desire to reach for the stars is ambitious. The desire to reach hearts is wise."

"A friend may be waiting behind a stranger's face."

"When you know better you do better."

"Still I'll rise."

"You may encounter many defeats, but you must not be defeated. In fact, it may be necessary to encounter the defeats, so you can know who you are, what you can rise from, how you can still come out of it."

"As soon as healing takes place, go out and heal somebody else."

"If you're going to live, leave a legacy. Make a mark on the world that can't be erased."

"But still, like air, I'll rise."

"I've learned that even when I have pains, I don't have to be one."

"Making a living is not the same thing as making a life."

"You may not control all the events that happen to you, but you can decide not to be reduced by them."

"As a nurse, we have the opportunity to heal the heart, mind, soul and body of our patients, their families and ourselves. They may not remember your name but they will never forget the way you made them feel."

"I can be changed by what happens to me, but I refuse to be reduced by it."

"First best is falling in love. Second best is being in love. Least best is falling out of love. But any of it is better than never having been in love."

"I am a Woman Phenomenally. Phenomenal Woman, that's me."

"I come as one, but stand as 10,000."

"You alone are enough. You have nothing to prove to anybody."

"There is a very fine line between loving life and being greedy for it."

"Every journey begins with a single step."

"If you find it in your heart to care for somebody else, you will have succeeded."

"You only are free when you realize you belong no place – you belong every place – no place at all. The price is high. The reward is great."

"You may shoot me with your words, you may cut me with your eyes, you may kill me with your hatefulness, but still, like air, I'll rise!"

"When you learn, teach, when you get, give."

"Be present in all things and thankful for all things."

"I did then what I knew how to do. Now that I know better, I do better."

"Hate, it has caused a lot of problems in the world, but has not solved one yet."

"Music was my refuge. I could crawl into the space between the notes and curl my back to loneliness."

"No matter what happens, or how bad it seems today, life does go on, and it will be better tomorrow."

"We delight in the beauty of the butterfly, but rarely admit the changes it has gone through to achieve that beauty."

"Hoping for the best, prepared for the worst, and unsurprised by anything in between."

"When someone shows you who they are, believe them the first time. People know themselves much better than you do. That's why it's important to stop expecting them to be something other than who they are."

"Hope and fear cannot occupy the same space. Invite one to stay."

"History, despite its wrenching pain, cannot be unlived, but if faced with courage, need not be lived again."

"Surviving is important. Thriving is elegant."

"This is a wonderful day, I have never seen this one before."

"One isn't necessarily born with courage, but one is born with potential. Without courage, we cannot practice any other virtue with consistency. We can't be kind, true, merciful, generous, or honest."

"Love recognizes no barriers. It jumps hurdles, leaps fences, penetrates walls to arrive at its destination full of hope."

"The ache for home lives in all of us. The safe place where we can go as we are and not be questioned."

"You will face many defeats in your life, but never let yourself be defeated."

"Courage is the most important of all the virtues because without courage, you can't practice any other virtue consistently."

"Life is going to give you just what you put in it. Put your whole heart in everything you do, and pray, then you can wait."

"A woman's heart should be so hidden in God that a man has to seek Him just to find her."

"And when great souls die, after a period peace blooms, slowly and always irregularly. Spaces fill with a kind of soothing electric vibration. Our senses, restored, never to be the same, whisper to us. They existed. They existed. We can be. Be and be better. For they existed."

"Love life. Engage in it. Give it all you've got. Love it with a passion because life truly does give back, many times over, what you put into it."

"If I am not good to myself, how can I expect anyone else to be good to me?"

"Everything in the universe has a rhythm, everything dances."

"It is time for parents to teach young people early on that in diversity there is beauty and there is strength."

"In all the world, there is no heart for me like yours. In all the world, there is no love for you like mine."

"You may write me down in history With your bitter, twisted lies. You may trod me in the very dirt, but still like dust, I'll rise."

"Most people don't grow up. Most people age. They find parking spaces, honor their credit cards, get married, have children, and call that maturity. What that is, is aging."

"We all should know that diversity makes for a rich tapestry, and we must understand that all the threads of the tapestry are equal in value no matter what their color."

"If you have only one smile in you give it to the people you love."

"I want to thank you, Lord, for life and all that's in it. Thank you for the day and for the hour, and the minute."

"I think a hero is any person really intent on making this a better place for all people."

"Let gratitude be the pillow upon which you kneel to say your nightly prayer. And let faith be the bridge you build to overcome evil and welcome good."

"When we give cheerfully and accept gratefully, everyone is blessed."

"To those who are given much, much is expected."

"Each time a woman stands up for herself, without knowing it possibly, without claiming it, she stands up for all women."

"The need for change bulldozed a road down the center of my mind."

"I don't trust anyone who doesn't laugh."

"I've learned that you shouldn't go through life with a catcher's mitt on both hands; you need to be able to throw something back."

"Bitterness is like cancer. It eats."

"If you have only one smile in you, give it to the people you love. Don't be surly at home, then go out in the street and start grinning 'Good morning' at total strangers."

"I've learned that whenever I decide something with an open heart, I usually make the right decision."

"Freedom is never free."

"If one is lucky, a solitary fantasy can totally transform one million realities."

"Open your eyes to the beauty around you, open your mind to the wonders of life, open your heart to those who love you, and always be true to yourself."

"While I know myself as a creation of God, I am also obligated to realize and remember that everyone else and everything else are also God's creation."

"Love is like a virus. It can happen to anybody at any time."

"Anything that works against you can also work for you once you understand the Principle of Reverse."

"The problem I have with haters is that they see my glory, but they don't know my story..."

"Life is pure adventure, and the sooner we realize that, the quicker we will be able to treat life as art."

"A Woman in harmony with her spirit is like a river flowing. She goes where she will without pretense and arrives at her destination prepared to be herself and only herself."

"Each person deserves a day away in which no problems are confronted, no solutions searched for."

"A great soul serves everyone all the time. A great soul never dies. It brings us together again and again."

"Stepping onto a brand-new path is difficult, but not more difficult than remaining in a situation, which is not nurturing to the whole woman."

"A woman who is convinced that she deserves to accept only the best challenges herself to give the best. Then she is living phenomenally."

"Develop enough courage so that you can stand up for yourself and then stand up for somebody else."

"You may encounter many defeats, but you must not be defeated. Please remember that your difficulties do not define you. They simply strengthen your ability to overcome."

"Don't let the man bring you down."

"No one can take the place of a friend, no one."

"We are only as blind as we want to be."

"We spend precious hours fearing the inevitable. It would be wise to use that time adoring our families, cherishing our friends and living our lives."

"My great hope is to laugh as much as I cry; to get my work done and try to love somebody and have the courage to accept the love in return."

"Bitterness is like cancer. It eats upon the host. But anger is like fire. It burns it all clean."

"Some people cannot see a good thing when it is right here, right now. Others can sense a good thing coming when it is days, months, or miles away."

"Poetry puts starch in your backbone so you can stand, so you can compose your life."

"Each of us, famous or infamous, is a role model for somebody, and if we aren't, we should behave as though we are – cheerful, kind, loving, courteous. Because you can be sure someone is watching and taking deliberate and diligent notes."

"There's a world of difference between truth and facts. Facts can obscure truth."

"We are more alike than unalike."

"There is nothing so pitiful as a young cynic because he has gone from knowing nothing to believing nothing."

"Living well is an art that can be developed: a love of life and ability to take great pleasure from small offerings and assurance that the world owes you nothing and that every gift is exactly that, a gift."

"Have enough courage to trust love one more time and always one more time."

"While one may encounter many defeats, one must not be defeated."

"The main thing in one's own private world is to try to laugh as much as you cry."

"People will never forget how you made them feel."

"My wish for you is that you continue. Continue to be who and how you are, to astonish a mean world with your acts of kindness."

"At our best, we are all teachers."

"It is this belief in a power larger than myself and other than myself which allows me to venture into the unknown and even the unknowable."

"Stand up straight and realize who you are, that you tower over your circumstances. You are a child of God. Stand up straight."

"You may not remember what a person said to you, you may not remember what a person did to you, but you will never forget how a person made you feel!"

"Difficult is a far cry from impossible. The distance between these two lies hope. Hope and fear cannot occupy the same space at the same time. Invite one to stay."

"I am the dream and the hope of the slave."

"If you must look back, do so forgivingly. If you will look forward, do so prayerfully. But the wisest course would be to be present in the present gratefully."

"I believe that one can never leave home. I believe that one carries the shadows, the dreams, the fears and the dragons of home under one's skin, at the extreme corners of one's eyes and possibly in the gristle of the earlobe."

"The horizon leans forward, offering you space to place new steps of change."

"Whining is not only graceless, but can be dangerous. It can alert a brute that a victim is in the neighborhood."

"When women take care of their health they become their own best friend."

"Courage allows the successful woman to fail – and to learn powerful lessons from the failure – so that in the end, she didn't fail at all."

"I would like to be known as an intelligent woman, a courageous woman, a loving woman, a woman who teaches by being."

"Women should be tough, tender, laugh as much as possible, and live long lives."

"Just like moons and suns, With certainty of tides, Just like hopes springing high, Still I'll rise."

"Seek patience and passion in equal amounts. Patience alone will not build the temple. Passion alone will destroy its walls."

"Bringing the gifts that my ancestors gave, I am the dream and the hope of the slave. I rise. I rise. I rise."

"A wise woman wishes to be no one's enemy; a wise woman refuses to be anyone's victim."

"Ritie, don't worry 'cause you ain't pretty. Plenty pretty women I seen digging ditches or worse. You smart. I swear to God, I rather you have a good mind than a cute behind."

"Beneath the skin, beyond the differing features and into the true heart of being, fundamentally, we are more alike, my friend, than we are unalike."

"If you are going down a road and don't like what's in front of you, and look behind you and don't like what you see, get off the road. Create a new path!"

"I believe most plain girls are virtuous because of the scarcity of opportunity to be otherwise."

"When we cast our bread upon the waters we can presume that someone downstream whose face we will never know will benefit from our action, as we who are downstream from another will profit from the grantor's gift."

"The real difficulty is to overcome how you think about yourself."

"I want to be a good human being. I'm doing my best, and I'm working at it."

"We can learn to see each other and see ourselves in each other and recognize that human beings are more alike than we are unalike."

"We need Joy as we need air. We need Love as we need water. We need each other as we need the earth we share."

"I always felt, if I can get to a library, I'll be OK."

"Love liberates; it doesn't bind."

"Thank you, always say thank you; it's the greatest gift you can give someone; because thank you is what you say to God."

"I have a son, who is my heart. A wonderful young man, daring and loving and strong and kind."

"Life sometimes gives you a second chance."

"I sustain myself with the love of family."

"Nothing succeeds like success. Get a little success, and then just get a little more."

"You are the sum total of everything you've ever seen, heard, eaten, smelled, been told, forgot – it's all there. Everything influences each of us, and because of that I try to make sure that my experiences are positive."

"I've got a magic charm That I keep up my sleeve, I can walk the ocean floor And never have to breathe."

"God puts rainbows in the clouds so that each of us – in the dreariest and most dreaded moments – can see a possibility of hope."

"Lord keep Your arm around my shoulder and Your hand over my mouth."

"We cannot change the past, but we can change our attitude toward it. Uproot guilt and plant forgiveness. Tear out arrogance and seed humility. Exchange love for hate – thereby, making the present comfortable and the future promising."

"I learned a long time ago the wisest thing I can do is be on my own side, be an advocate for myself and others like me."

"I have heard it said that winter, too, will pass, that spring is a sign that summer is due at last. See, all we have to do is hang on."

"The truth is, no one of us can be free until everybody is free."

"The more you know of your history, the more liberated you are."

"If it is true that a chain is only as strong as its weakest link, isn't it also true a society is only as healthy as its sickest citizen and only as wealthy as its most deprived?"

"Let choice whisper in your ear and love murmur in your heart. Be ready. Here comes life."

"Don't bring negative to my door."

"I must undertake to love myself and to respect myself as though my very life depends upon self-love and self-respect."

"A leader sees greatness in other people. He nor she can be much of a leader if all she sees is herself."

"Listen to yourself and in that quietude you might hear the voice of God."

"Poetry is music written for the human voice."

"Strong women- precious jewels all- their humanness is evident in their accessibility. We are able to enter into the spirit of these women and rejoice in their warmth and courage."

"I'm a feminist. I've been a female for a long time now. It'd be stupid not to be on my own side."

"The caged bird sings with a fearful trill, of things unknown, but longed for still, and his tune is heard on the distant hill, for the caged bird sings of freedom."

"My mother is so full of joy and life. I am her child. And that is better than being the child of anyone else in the world."

"I think we all have empathy. We may not have enough courage to display it."

"Words mean more than what is set down on paper. It takes the human voice to infuse them with shades of deeper meaning."

"My mission in life is not merely to survive, but to thrive."

"I have great respect for the past. If you don't know where you've come from, you don't know where you're going. I have respect for the past, but I'm a person of the moment. I'm here, and I do my best to be completely centered at the place I'm at, then I go forward to the next place."

"I am a child of God. I always carry that with me."

"Having courage does not mean that we are unafraid. Having courage and showing courage mean we face our fears. We are able to say, 'I have fallen, but I will get up.'"

"Love liberates. Love – not sentimentality, not mush – but true love gives you enough courage that you can say to somebody, "Don't do that, baby." And the person will know you're not preaching but teaching."

"Still, when it looked like the sun wasn't going to shine anymore, God put a rainbow in the clouds."

"No one comes from the earth like grass. We come like trees. We all have roots."

"I know why the caged bird sings."

"If I could give you one thought, it would be to lift someone up. Lift a stranger up – lift her up. I would ask you, mother and father, brother and sister, lovers, mother and daughter, father and son, lift someone. The very idea of lifting someone up will lift you, as well."

"When you know you are of worth, you don't have to raise your voice, you don't have to become rude, you don't have to become vulgar; you just are. And you are like the sky is, as the air is, the same way water is wet. It doesn't have to protest."

"You build your 'COURAGE MUSCLE' daily, by being courageous in little things. Just do right..."

"Love is many things. It is varied. One thing love is not, is unsure."

"Each of us needs to withdraw from the cares which will not withdraw from us. We need hours of aimless wandering or spates of time sitting on park benches, observing the mysterious world of ants and the canopy of treetops."

"Only equals make friends, every other relationship is contrived and off balance."

"My son is the best thing that ever happened to me. And through me – to a lot of people."

"She comprehended the perversity of life, that in the struggle lies the joy."

"The area where we are the greatest is the area in which we inspire, encourage and connect with another human being."

"Its not where your dreams take you, its where you take your dreams."

"Light and shadow are opposite sides of the same coin. We can illuminate our paths or darken our way. It is a matter of choice."

"Hope is born again in the faces of children."

"I work very hard, and I play very hard. I'm grateful for life. And I live it – I believe life loves the liver of it. I live it."

"Human beings are more alike than unalike, and what is true anywhere is true everywhere, yet I encourage travel to as many destinations as possible for the sake of education as well as pleasure."

"Alone, all alone Nobody, but nobody Can make it out here alone."

"Determine to live life with flair and laughter."

"We need much less than we think we need."

"I believe that every person is born with talent."

"We are all human; therefore, nothing human can be alien to us."

"I encourage you to live with life. Be courageous, adventurous. Give us a tomorrow, more than we deserve."

"You can never go home again, but the truth is you can never leave home, so it's all right."

"We are not our brother's keeper we are our brother and we are our sister. We must look past complexion and see community."

"No sun outlasts its sunset, but will rise again and bring the dawn."

"The thorn from the bush one has planted, nourished and pruned pricks more deeply and draws more blood."

"This is my life. it is my one time to be me. i want to experience every good thing."

"Mostly, what I have learned so far about aging, despite the creakiness of one's bones and cragginess of one's once-silken skin, is this: Do it. By all means, do it."

"You have to have courage to love somebody. Because you risk everything. Everything."

"A joyful spirit is evidence of a grateful heart."

"If we lose love and self respect for each other, this is how we finally die."

"The idea is to write it so that people hear it and it slides through the brain and goes straight to the heart."

"Love liberates. It doesn't just hold, that's ego. Love liberates."

"Make every effort to change things you do not like. If you cannot make a change, change the way you have been thinking. You might find a new solution."

"Forgive yourself – no one else will."

"If you have, give. If you learn, teach."

"Precious jewel, you glow, you shine, reflecting all the good things in the world. Just look at yourself."

"Nothing hurts more than realizing they meant everything to you, but you meant nothing to them."

"The nice thing about HOPE is that you can give it to someone else, someone who needs it even more than you do, and you will find you have not given yours away at all."

"Take a day to heal from the lies you've told yourself and the ones that have been told to you."

"My work is to be honest. My work is to try to think clearly, then have the courage to make sure that what I say is the truth."

"A person is the product of their dreams. So make sure to dream great dreams. And then try to live your dream."

"Being a woman is hard work."

"Give yourself time just to be with yourself."

"It's the fire in my eyes, And the flash of my teeth, The swing in my waist, And the joy in my feet. I'm a woman Phenomenally."

"Here on the pulse of this new day You may have the grace to look up and out And into your sister's eyes, Into your brother's face, your country

And say simply Very simply With hope Good morning."

"I am not competing with anyone other than myself. I want to be excellent at whatever I do."

"I respect myself and insist upon it from everybody. And because I do it, I then respect everybody, too."

"My hope is that we develop enough courage to develop courage. To try to have, try to learn to treat each other fairly, with generosity and kindness."

"I try to see every day as a celebration."

"Everyone grows old but not everyone grows up."

"I am a woman phenomenally, phenomenal woman that is your grandmother, that is your mother, that is your sister, that is you and that is me."

"The happy heart runs with the river, floats on the air, lifts to the music, soars with the eagle, hopes with the prayer."

"I will look after you and I will look after anybody you say needs to be looked after, any way you say. I am here. I brought my whole self to you. I am your mother."

"Happiness is a chance to talk to a friend, to hear good music, to have a good glass of wine. Happiness is a chance to be myself and to find people with whom I agree or who I don't agree but I can learn something."

"A mother's love liberates."

"When we find someone who is brave, fun, intelligent, and loving, we have to thank the universe."

"I believe that the most important single thing, beyond discipline and creativity is daring to dare."

"You forgive yourself for every failure because you are trying to do the right thing. God knows that and you know it. Nobody else may know it."

"Most people don't grow up. It's too damn difficult. What happens is most people get older."

"Age is nothing; waking up is everything."

"I have found that among its other benefits, giving liberates the soul of the giver."

"Life is a gift, and i try to respond with grace and courtesy."

"You rose into my life like a promised sunrise, brightening my days with the light in your eyes. I've never been so strong. Now I'm where I belong."

"Try to live your life in a way that you will not regret years of useless virtue and inertia and timidity."

"Life loves the liver of it. You must live and life will be good to you."

"As long as you're breathing, it's never too late to do some good."

"Love heals. Heals and liberates. I use the word love, not meaning sentimentality, but a condition so strong that it may be that which holds the stars in their heavenly positions and that which causes the blood to flow orderly in our veins."

"Perhaps travel cannot prevent bigotry, but by demonstrating that all peoples cry, laugh, eat, worry, and die, it can introduce the idea that if we try and understand each other, we may even become friends."

"We all have that possibility, that potential and that promise of seeing beyond the seeming."

"There is no place where God is not."

"How important it is for us to recognize and celebrate our heroes and she-roes!"

"In order to win, we pay with energy and effort and discipline. If we lose, we pay in disappointment, discontent, and lack of fulfillment."

"All God's children need traveling shoes."

"I will write on the pages of history what I want them to say. I will be myself. I will speak my own name."

"Hope for the best, be prepared for the worse. Life is shocking, but you must never appear to be shocked. For no matter how bad it is it could be worse and no matter how good it is it could be better."

"We must create a climate where people agree that human beings are more alike than unalike. The only way to do that is through education."

"Every day I awaken I am grateful. My intent is to be totally present in that day. And laugh as much as possible."

"I'm grateful for being here, for being able to think, for being able to see, for being able to taste, for appreciating love – for knowing that it exists in a world so rife with vulgarity, with brutality and violence, and yet love exists. I'm grateful to know that it exists."

"The woman who survives intact and happy must be at once tender and tough."

"If you're for the right thing, you do it without thinking."

"Faith is the evidence of the unseen."

"Life loves the liver of it."

"Spirit is an invisible force made visible in all life."

"If I'm here, I'll be trying to be a better human being, a better writer, a better friend and a better beloved."

"Family isn't always blood. It's the people in your life who want you in theirs. The ones who accept you for who you are. The ones who would do anything to see you smile, and who love you no matter what."

"The most important thing is to DARE."

"If I have a monument in this world, it is my son."

"Be certain that you do not die without having done something wonderful for humanity."

"Intelligence always had a pornographic influence on me."

"And I not only have the right to stand up for myself, but I have the responsibility. I can't ask somebody else to stand up for me if I won't stand up for myself. And once you stand up for yourself, you'd be surprised that people say, "Can I be of help?""

"I've learned that regardless of your relationship with your parents, you'll miss them when they're gone from your life."

"Dare to let your dreams reach beyond you."

"Laugh and dare to try to love somebody, starting with yourself. You must love yourself first, of course, and you must protect yourself so that nobody overrides you, overrules you, or steps on you. Just say, 'Just a minute. I'm worth everything, dear.'"

"Whether you are happy or whether you are sad, it is wise to remember you are really in process."

"You may encounter many defeats, but you must not be defeated. In fact, the encountering may be the very experience which creates the vitality and the power to endure."

"Look what you've already come through! Don't deny it. Say I'm stronger than I thought I was."

"I don't trust any revolution where love is not allowed."

"It's true. I can do anything and do it well because God loves me. It still humbles me."

"Poetry gave me back my voice."

"I'm convinced of this: Good done anywhere is good done everywhere. For a change, start by speaking to people rather than walking by them like they're stones that don't matter. As long as you're breathing, it's never too late to do some good."

"I want all my senses engaged. Let me absorb the world's variety and uniqueness."

"You can never be great at anything unless you love it."

"Since time is the one immaterial object which we cannot influence neither speed up nor slow down add to nor diminish it is an imponderably valuable gift."

"Each of us has that right, that possibility, to invent ourselves daily. If a person does not invent herself, she will be invented. So, to be bodacious enough to invent ourselves is wise."

"The truth is very important. No matter how negative it is, it is imperative that you learn the truth, not necessarily the facts. I mean, that, that can come, but facts can stand in front of the truth and almost obscure the truth. It is imperative that students learn the truth of our history."

"My life has been one great big joke, A dance that's walked, A song that's spoke, I laugh so hard I almost choke, When I think about myself."

"It is only out of ignorance that people are cruel, because they really don't think it will come back."

"Every person needs to take one day away. A day in which one consciously separates the past from the future."

"Eating is so intimate. It's very sensual. When you invite someone to sit at your table and you want to cook for them, you're inviting a person into your life."

"I long, as does every human being, to be at home wherever I find myself."

"I think I know that I deserve better. And so I try for better. I'm never so put off that I would ever walk out of a place not having tried the best I could."

"Does my sexiness upset you? Does it come as a surprise That I dance like I've got diamonds At the meeting of my thighs?"

"Don't get older just to get wiser. If you get older, you will be wiser, I believe that – if you dare. But get older because it's fun!"

"It is sad but true that sometimes we need the tragedy to help us to see how human we are and how we are more alike than we are different."

"Time itself is an individual gift. It is wise to cherish it carefully and give it away generously."

"When I look back, I am so impressed again with the life-giving power of literature. If I were a young person today, trying to gain a sense of myself in the world, I would do that again by reading, just as I did when I was young."

"Prejudice is a burden that confuses the past, threatens the future and renders the present inaccessible."

"Stormy or sunny days, glorious or lonely nights, I maintain an attitude of gratitude."

"Step off the road. Build yourself a brand new path."

"I've learned that every day you should reach out and touch someone. People love a warm hug, or just a friendly pat on the back."

"Elimination of illiteracy is as serious an issue to our history as the abolition of slavery."

"It may in fact be utterly impossible to be successful without helping others to become successful."

"Each of us has the power and responsibility to become a rainbow in the clouds."

"I'm a spring leaf trembling in anticipation."

"One must learn to care for oneself first, so that one can then dare to care for someone else."

"At 50, I began to know who I was. It was like waking up to myself."

"The honorary duty of a human being is to love."

"One must know not just how to accept a gift, but with what grace to share it."

"The future is plump with promise."

"Life loves to be taken by the lapel and told: 'I'm with you kid. Let's go.'"

"I'm convinced of this: Good done anywhere is good done everywhere."

"I know for sure that loves saves me and that it is here to save us all."

"You think you may not be heard. Speak anyway."

"All great artists draw from the same resource: the human heart, which tells us that we are all more alike than we are unalike."

"Just as hope rings through laughter, it can also shine through tears."

"Any book that helps a child to form a habit of reading, to make reading one of his deep and continuing needs, is good for him."

"I agreed a long time ago, I would not live at any cost. If I am moved or forced away from what I think is the right thing, I will not do it."

"It is a no-fail, incontrovertible reality: If you get, give. If you learn, teach. You can't do anything with that except do it."

"We may act sophisticated and worldly but I believe we feel safest when we go inside ourselves and find home, a place where we belong and maybe the only place we really do."

"I think the more we know the better we are. I mean not just facts. The more we know about each other, the closer we are to learn something about our selves."

"To describe my mother would be to write about a hurricane in its perfect power. Or the climbing, falling colors of a rainbow."

"You may be pretty or plain, heavy or thin, gay or straight, poor or rich. But remember this: In an election, every voice is equally powerful – don't underestimate your vote. Voting is the great equalizer."

"All my work, my life, everything I do is about survival, not just bare, awful, plodding survival, but survival with grace and faith. While one may encounter many defeats, one must not be defeated."

"If we are honest and fair, then we are known by that. If we are not, alas, we are known by that as well. What we want to do is do right, but you have to say it, you have to show it, and not stop."

"The children to whom we read simple stories may or may not show gratitude, but each boon we give strengthens the pillars of the world."

"Raising kids is like nailing Jell-O to a tree."

"I think when we don't know what to do it's wise to do nothing. Sit down quietly; quiet our hearts and minds and breathe deeply."

"Every experience shapes your writing, being stuck in a car on a lonely bridge, or dancing at a prom, being the it girl on the beach, all of those things influence your life, they influence how you write, and the topics you choose to write about."

"Sometimes all you need in love is to make each other happy, to make each other laugh. So long as you can still do that ten years down the line then I think you're gold. Never let the laughter slip from your relationship."

"All knowledge is spendable currency, depending on the market."

"When I forgive other people, I let them go, I free them from my ignorance. And as soon as I do, I feel lighter, brighter and better."

"The idea of overcoming is always fascinating to me. It's fascinating because few of us realize how much energy we have expended just to be here today. I don't think we give ourselves enough credit for the overcoming."

"I love the song 'I Hope You Dance' by Lee Ann Womack. I was going to write that song, but someone beat me to it."

"Love is that condition in the human spirit so profound that it allows me to survive, and better than that, to thrive with passion, compassion, and style."

"Because of our routines we forget that life is an ongoing adventure."

"People feel guilty. And guilt is stymieing. Guilt immobilizes. Guilt closes the air ducts and the veins, and makes people ignorant."

"We will sometimes have defeats in life but you can have defeats without being defeated, you could fail without being a failure. When you see failure and defeats as merely part of the process to get to when."

"When we decide to be happy we accept the responsibility to bring happiness to someone else."

"Everybody is worth everything."

"Take a month and show some kindness for the folks who thought that blindness was an illness that affected eyes alone."

"Don't let anybody raise you. You've been raised."

"My grandmother told me that every good thing I do helps some human being in the world. I believed her 50 years ago and still do."

"The human heart is so delicate and sensitive that it always needs some tangible encouragement to prevent it from faltering in its labour."

"Look heavenward and speak the word aloud. Peace. We look at our world and speak the word aloud. Peace."

"There's racism and sexism and ageism and all sorts of idiocies. But bad news is not news. We've had bad news as a species for a long time. We've had slavery and human sacrifice and the holocaust and brutalities of such measure."

"Tell the truth and not the facts."

"The best comfort food will always be greens, cornbread, and fried chicken."

"My life has been long, and believing that life loves the liver of it, I have dared to try many things, sometimes trembling, but daring still."

"Don't let the incidents which take place in life bring you low. And certainly don't whine. You can be brought low, that's OK, but don't be reduced by them. Just say, 'That's life.'"

"You can only become great at something you are willing to sacrifice for."

"Poetry helps my soul escape its encasement."

"It's amazing. I can do anything. And do it well. Any good thing, I can do it. That's why I am who I am, yes, because God loves me and I'm amazed at it. I'm grateful for it."

"Hold those things that tell your history and protect them."

"Without courage, we cannot practice any other virtue with consistency."

"Love is that condition in the human spirit so profound that it empowers us to develop courage; to trust that courage and build bridges with it; to trust those bridges and cross over them so we can attempt to reach each other."

"The real difficulty is to overcome how you think about yourself. If we don't have that we never grow, we never learn, and sure as heck we should never teach."

"Education is a process that goes on 'til death. The moment you see someone who knows she has found the one true way, and can call all the others false, then you know you're in the company of an ignoramus."

"There is a spirit in all music, the spirit has the ability to conjure up thoughts even pictures of something that happened or you wished would happen or you anticipate happening. Music has the ability to create ideas in you and me. It has the ability to encourage us to be creative."

"If we all hold on to the mistake, we can't see our own glory in the mirror because we have the mistake between our faces and the mirror; we can't see what we're capable of being. You can ask forgiveness of others, but in the end the real forgiveness is in one's own self."

"My greatest blessing has been the birth of my son. My next greatest blessing has been my ability to turn people into children of mine."

"Modesty is a learned affectation. It's no good. Humility is great, because humility says, 'There was someone before me. I'm following in somebody's footsteps.'"

"It is important that we learn humility, which says there was someone else before me who paid for me. My responsibility is to prepare myself so that I can pay for someone else who is yet to come."

"Education helps one case cease being intimidated by strange situations."

"Life is a glorious banquet, a limitless and delicious buffet."

"The quality of strength lined with tenderness is an unbeatable combination, as are intelligence and necessity when unblunted by formal education."

"If our children are to approve of themselves, they must see that we approve of ourselves."

"Women should be tough, tender, laugh as much as possible, and live long lives. The struggle for equality continues unabated, and the woman warrior who is armed with wit and courage will be among the first to celebrate victory."

"I am capable of what every other human is capable of. This is one of the great lessons of war and life ."

"I'm just someone who likes cooking and for whom sharing food is a form of expression."

"If we are bold, love strikes away the chains of fear from our souls."

"We have it in us to be splendid."

"Let us live so we do not regret years of inertia and ignorance, so when we die we can say all of our energy was dedicated to the noble liberation of the human mind and spirit, beginning with my own."

"If I insist on being pessimistic, there is always tomorrow. Today I am blessed."

"The best candy shop a child can be left alone in, is the library."

"Rainbows are people whose lives are bright, shining examples for others."

"Shakespeare must be a black girl."

"In spite of everything that was done to me and my race, in spite of the adversity and the bitter moments, again we rise."

"If we don't plant the right things, we will reap the wrong things. It goes without saying. And you don't have to be, you know, a brilliant biochemist and you don't have to have an IQ of 150. Just common sense tells you to be kind, ninny, fool. Be kind."

"My pride had been starched by a family who assumed unlimited authority in its own affairs."

"Love is a condition so powerful; it may be that which pulls the stars in the firmament. It may be that which pushes and urges the blood in the veins. Courage: you have to have courage to love somebody because you risk everything-ever ything."

"If you have a song to sing, who are you not to open your mouth and sing to the world?"

"I refuse to allow any man-made differences to separate me from any other human beings."

"When I was asked to do something good, I often say yes, I'll try, yes, I'll do my best. And part of that is believing, if God loves me, if God made everything from leaves to seals and oak trees, then what is it I can't do?"

"Once you appreciate one of your blessings, one of your senses, your sense of hearing, then you begin to respect the sense of seeing and touching and tasting, you learn to respect all the senses."

"Be wary when a naked person offers you his shirt."

"We have to confront ourselves. Do we like what we see in the mirror? And, according to our light, according to our understanding, according to our courage, we will have to say yea or nay – and rise!"

"It's one of the greatest gifts you can give yourself, to forgive. Forgive everybody."

"The plague of racism is insidious, entering into our minds as smoothly and quietly and invisibly as floating airborne microbes enter into our bodies to find lifelong purchase in our bloodstreams."

"In order to be profoundly dishonest, a person must have one of two qualities: either he is unscrupulously ambitious, or he is unswervingly egocentric."

"This is what I am learning, at 82 years old: the main thing is to be in love with the search for truth."

"You're not serious; you're boring as hell."

"Every Day you should reach out and touch someone."

"To be human is to be challenged to be more divine. Not even to try to meet such a challenge is the biggest defeat imaginable."

"Let the brain go to work, let it meet the heart and you will be able to forgive."

"All men are prepared to accomplish the incredible if their ideals are threatened."

"We need to remember that we are all created creative and can invent new scenarios as frequently as they are needed."

"That knowledge humbles me, melts my bones, closes my ears, and makes my teeth rock loosely in their gums. And it also liberates me. I am a big bird winging over high mountains, down into serene valleys. I am ripples of waves on silver seas. I'm a spring leaf trembling in anticipation."

"Love recognizes no barriers."

"We allow our ignorance to prevail upon us and make us think we can survive alone, alone in patches, alone in groups, alone in races, even alone in genders."

"Yet it is only love which sets us free."

"Nature has no mercy at all. Nature says, "I'm going to snow. If you have on a bikini and no snowshoes, that's tough. I am going to snow anyway.""

"Sisterhood means if you happen to be in Burma and I happen to be in San Diego and I'm married to someone who is very jealous and you're married to somebody who is very possessive, if you call me in the middle of the night, I have to come."

"Listen carefully to what country people call mother wit. In those homely sayings are couched the collective wisdom of generations."

"I am convinced that words are things, and we simply don't have the machinery to measure what they are. I believe that words are tangible things..."

"Leaving behind nights of terror and fear, I rise. Into a daybreak that's wondrously clear, I rise."

"In a world so rife with vulgarity, with brutality and violence, love exists. I'm grateful to know that it exists."

"I believe in living a poetic life, an art full life. Everything we do from the way we raise our children to the way we welcome our friends is part of a large canvas we are creating."

"Everybody born comes from the Creator trailing wisps of glory. We come from the Creator with creativity. I think that each one of us is born with creativity."

"When I look back, I am so impressed again with the life-giving power of literature."

"Easy reading is damn hard writing. But if it's right, it's easy. It's the other way round, too. If it's slovenly written, then it's hard to read. It doesn't give the reader what the careful writer can give the reader."

"Jealousy in romance is like salt in food. A little can enhance the savor, but too much can spoil the pleasure and, under certain circumstances, can be life-threatening."

"In an unfamiliar culture, it is wise to offer no innovations, no suggestions, or lessons."

"In so many ways, segregation shaped me, and education liberated me."

"When I'm writing, I write. And then it's as if the muse is convinced that I'm serious and says, 'Okay. Okay. I'll come.'"

"Be courageous, but not foolhardy. Walk proud as you are."

"You can't forgive without loving. And I don't mean sentimentality. I don't mean mush. I mean having enough courage to stand up and say, 'I forgive. I'm finished with it.'"

"If we live long enough, we may even get over war. I imagine a time when somebody will mention the word war and everyone in the room will start to laugh. And what do you mean war?"

"While the rest of the world has been improving technology, Ghana has been improving the quality of man's humanity to man."

"Pretty Women Wonder Where My Secret Lies, Im Not Cute Or Built To Fit A Fashion Models Size."

"Everyone has at least one story, and each of us is funny if we admit it. You have to admit you're the funniest person you've ever heard of."

"Continue to plant a kiss of concern on the cheek of the sick and the aged and infirm and count that actions as natural and to be expected."

"When people see the laughing face, even if they're jealous of it, their burden is lightened. But do it first for yourself. Laugh and dare to try to love somebody, starting with yourself."

"I am a very religious person, so it is the presence of God, the constant unwavering, unrelenting presence of God which continues to help me to keep a character which I am proud to show."

"Let me tell so much truth. I want to tell the truth in my work. The truth will lead me to all."

"We must be warriors in the struggle against ignorance."

"When things were very bad his soul just crawled behind his heart and curled up and went to sleep."

"I'm young as morning and fresh as dew. Everybody loves me and so do you."

"I'm grateful to be an American. I am grateful that we can be angry at the terrorist assault and at the same time be intelligent enough not to hold a grudge against every Arab and every Muslim."

"Each of us has a responsibility for being alive: one responsibility to creation, of which we are a part, another to the creator a debt we repay by trying to extend our areas of comprehension."

"Home is that youthful region where a child is the only real living inhabitant. Parents, siblings, and neighbors are mysterious apparitions who come, go, and do strange unfathomable thing in and around the child, the region's only enfranchised citizen."

"You have to develop ways so that you can take up for yourself, and then you take up for someone else. And so sooner or later, you have enough courage to really stand up for the human race and say, 'I'm a representative. '"

"If more Africans had eaten missionaries, the continent would be in better shape."

"Having courage does not mean we are unafraid."

"I admire people who dare to take the language, English, and understand it and understand the melody."

"I dreamt we walked together along the shore. We made satisfying small talk and laughed. This morning I found sand in my shoe and a seashell in my pocket. Was I only dreaming?"

"Children's talent to endure stems from their ignorance of alternatives."

"Language. I loved it. And for a long time I would think of myself, of my whole body, as an ear."

"When the human race neglects its weaker members, when the family neglects its weakest one – it's the first blow in a suicidal movement."

"Don't hesitate to learn the most painful aspects of our history, understand it."

"It's hard because people think they have something to lose and the truth is they have everything to gain in trying to love somebody."

"It is imperative that young white men and women study the black

American history. It is imperative that blacks and whites study the Asian American history."

"And one of my absolute favorite quotes of all-time, one that I've adopted as one of my greatest life mottos: Life loves to be taken by the lapel and told: "I'm with you kid. Let's go.""

"And if a person is religious, I think it's good, it helps you a bit. But if you're not, at least you can have the sense that there is a condition inside you which looks at the stars with amazement and awe."

"I also wear a hat or a very tightly pulled head tie when I write. I suppose I hope by doing that I will keep my brains from seeping out of my scalp and running in great gray blobs down my neck, into my ears, and over my face."

"My mother said I must always be intolerant of ignorance but understanding of illiteracy."

"Hope does not take away your problems. It can lift you above them."

"To take a few nouns, and a few pronouns, and adverbs and

adjectives, and put them together, ball them up, and throw them against the wall to make them bounce. That's what Norman Mailer did. That's what James Baldwin did, and Joan Didion did, and that's what I do – that's what I mean to do."

"The truth will lead me to all."

"The writer has to take the most used, most familiar objects – nouns, pronouns, verbs, adverbs – ball them together and make them bounce, turn them a certain way and make people get into a romantic mood; and another way, into a bellicose mood. I'm most happy to be a writer."

"A bizarre sensation pervades a relationship of pretense. No truth seems true."

"I make writing as much a part of my life as I do eating or listening to music."

"As far as I knew white women were never lonely, except in books. White men adored them, Black men desired them and Black women worked for them."

"Courage, I don't think anybody is born with courage. I think you may be born with a flair to braggadocio, you know. That's not courage."

"Oh, the holiness of being the injured party."

"I like to go back and read poems that I wrote fifty years ago, twenty years ago, and sometimes they surprise me – I didn't know I knew that then. Or maybe I didn't know it then, and I know more now."

"Try, start always at home. This is my encouragement to all writers, start at home. All virtues and vices begin at home, and then spread abroad."

"I am grateful to be a woman. I must have done something great in another life."

"Intelligence is a separate gift, for the benefit of students, so that they may think of themselves as intellectual and not very intelligent, or intelligent and not very intellectual. One hopes, of course, that they try to bring the two virtues, the two elements, into their lives at the same time."

"I come as one but I stand as ten thousand."

"In a magazine, one can get – from cover to cover – 15 to 20 different ideas about life and how to live it."

"Money and power can liberate only if they are used to do so. They can imprison and inhibit more finally than barred windows and iron chains."

"The truth is you never can leave home. You take it with you everywhere you go. It's under your skin. It moves the tongue or slows it, colors the thinking, impedes upon the logic."

"A rose by any other name may smell as sweet, but a woman called by a devaluing name will only be weakened by the misnomer."

"I love a Hebrew National hot dog with an ice-cold Corona – no lime. If the phone rings, I won't answer until I'm done."

"The breezes of the West African night were intimate and shy, licking the hair, sweeping through cotton dresses with unseemly intimacy, then disappearing into the utter blackness."

"If growing up is painful for the Southern Black girl, being aware of her displacement is the rust on the razor that threatens the throat. It is an unnecessary insult."

"We are the victims of the world's most comprehensive robbery. Life demands a balance. It's all right if we do a little robbing now."

"To be left alone on the tightrope of youthful unknowing is to experience the excruciating beauty of full freedom and the threat of eternal indecision."

"The most called-upon prerequisite of a friend is an accessible ear."

"If men are God's gift to women, then God must really love gag gifts."

"Do not be wedded forever to fear, yoked eternally to brutishness."

"Independence is a heady draught, and if you drink it in your youth, it can have the same effect on the brain as young wine does. It does not matter that its taste is not always appealing. It is addictive and with each drink you want more."

"Few, if any, survive their teens. Most surrender to the vague but murderous pressure of adult conformity."

"Life offers us tickets to places which we have not knowingly asked for."

"When I passed forty I dropped pretense, 'cause men like women who got some sense."

"I know that I'm not the easiest person to live with. The challenge I put on myself is so great that the person I live with feels himself challenged. I bring a lot to bear, and I don't know how not to."

"In Stamps the segregation was so complete that most Black children didn't really, absolutely know what whites looked like."

"Now, after years of observation and enough courage to admit what I have observed, I try to plant peace if I do not want discord; to plant loyalty and honesty if I want to avoid betrayal and lies."

"Some critics will write 'Maya Angelou is a natural writer' – which is right after being a natural heart surgeon."

"The world had taken a deep breath and was having doubts about continuing to revolve."

"We must infuse our lives with art. Our national leaders must be informed that we want them to use our taxes to support street theatre in order to oppose street gangs. We should have a well-supported regional theatre in order to oppose regionalism and."

"Out of the huts of history's shame I rise."

"Anyone of us can be a rainbow in somebody's clouds. I want the University of Cincinnati to be a rainbow in the clouds. The University of Cincinnati is really a possibility of hope; it is a rainbow."

"I think that that's the wisest thing – to prevent illness before we try to cure something."

"Everything costs and costs the earth."

"He was a simple man who had no inferiority complex about his lack of education, and even more amazing no superiority complex because he had succeeded despite that lack."

"It's very important to know the neighbor next door and the people down the street and the people in another race."

"The black kids, the poor white kids, Spanish-speaking kids, and Asian kids in the US – in the face of everything to the contrary, they still bop and bump, shout and go to school somehow. Their optimism gives me hope."

"The Black female is assaulted in her tender years by all those common forces of nature at the same time she is caught in the tripartite crossfire of masculine prejudice, white illogical hate and Black lack of power."

"Creativity or talent, like electricity, is something I don't understand but something I'm able to harness and use."

"The first thing I do in the morning when I awaken is say, 'Thank you, Lord!' I'm grateful to be alive, and I'm going to try to tell the truth as well as I know and tell it as eloquently as I can so that people can hear it."

"Our stories come from our lives and from the playwright's pen, the mind of the actor, the roles we create, the artistry of life itself and the quest for peace."

"If a person – any human being – is told often enough, "You are nothing. You are nothing. You account for nothing. You count for nothing. You are less than a human being. I have no visibility of you", the person finally begins to believe it."

"When a person is going through hell, and she encounters someone who went through hellish hell and survived, then she can say, 'Mine is not so bad as all that. She came through, and so can I.'"

"Take the blinders from your vision take the padding from your ears and confess you've heard me crying and admit you've seen my tears."

"Sometimes guns really matter. Protecting those who need protection – children, women, minorities in rough parts of town, old folks living in places where cops aren't nearby. Guns are true empowerment for the powerless."

"Tragedy, no matter how sad, becomes boring to those not caught in its addictive caress."

"When it looks like the sun isn't going to shine any more, God puts a rainbow in the clouds. Each one of us has the possibility, the responsibility, the probability to be the rainbow in the clouds."

Afterword

As we close the pages of this collection, it's essential to pause and reflect on the lasting impact of Maya Angelou's words. Her quotes on success, education, and life are more than just inspirational—they are a testament to the power of the human spirit to overcome adversity, seek knowledge, and live with purpose.

Maya Angelou's life was a mosaic of experiences, each shaping her into the profound thinker, writer, and activist she became. Her words carry the weight of someone who not only observed the world but also actively engaged with it, transforming pain into poetry, struggle into strength, and hope into action.

Success, as Angelou reminds us, is not a destination but a journey. It's found in the courage to pursue one's dreams, the resilience to rise after every fall, and the wisdom to stay true to oneself. Through her reflections on education, Angelou encourages us to remain perpetual students of life, ever curious, ever open to learning. And in her musings on life, she offers us a guide to living authentically, with grace, compassion, and unwavering integrity.

This collection is more than just a compilation of quotes; it's a source of continual inspiration. Whether you are facing challenges, seeking motivation, or simply in need of a reminder that you are not alone in your journey, these words from Maya Angelou are here to uplift and guide you.

As you carry these quotes with you, remember that Angelou's wisdom is not confined to the pages of a book. It is a living, breathing force that you can draw upon whenever you need strength, clarity, or encouragement. Her legacy is a reminder that no matter where we come from, what obstacles we face, or what dreams we pursue, we have the power to rise above and create a life of meaning and purpose.

Thank you for taking this journey through the inspiring words of Maya Angelou. May her wisdom continue to resonate in your heart and mind, guiding you towards success, fostering your love for learning, and enriching your life.

Book from the Same Author

500 Best Quotes by Benjamin Franklin about Wisdom, Wealth, Achievements - https://www.amazon.com/dp/B0D87DZCMP

 500 Wise Quotes by Warren Buffett Investing, Income and Money- https://www.amazon.com/dp/B0D6P567D7

 500 Inspirational Quotes by Winston Churchill: About Attitude to Life, Success, and Purposefulness - https://www.amazon.com/dp/B0D2VBS8BK

500 Strong Motivational Quotes: Strong Quotes for Life - https://www.amazon.com/dp/B0D3FXGTKV

500 Valuable Quotes by Albert Einstein about Knowledge, Intelligence, Wealth - https://www.amazon.com/dp/B0D8YQ5XRP

500 Unique Quotes by Buddha about Life, Happiness, Death: Buddha Book of Quotes for Every day - https://www.amazon.com/dp/B0D97JDH3C

500 Inspirational Quotes by Rumi About Life, Love and Happiness: Book of Quotes by Rumi - https://www.amazon.com/dp/B0D9RZ67YM

500 Wisdom Quotes by Abraham Lincoln about Freedom, Responsibility and Democracy - https://www.amazon.com/dp/B0DC1HX148

500 Inspirational Quotes by Theodore Roosevelt about America, Education and Life - https://www.amazon.com/dp/B0DD2FM6BH

500 Motivational Quotes by Mark Twain about Money, Life and Love - https://www.amazon.com/dp/B0DDGZX13T

Made in the USA
Monee, IL
18 November 2024